Favourite Profanity

About the Author

The author of this collection likes to describe himself while holding a glass of red wine, legs crossed at the knees as optimistic and light-hearted, perhaps too much at times. Innocent? Ha! Definitely amusing. Possibly demented.

But when the wine was no more and I found myself alone, I wrote this collection. I want to share with you a look into my most intimate emotions, hoping that one of my poems might mean as much to you as it does to me. I hope you find it lovely.

Christiaan van Deventer

Favourite Profanity

Olympia Publishers
London

www.olympiapublishers.com
OLYMPIA PAPERBACK EDITION

Copyright © Christiaan van Deventer 2024

The right of Christiaan van Deventer to be identified as author of this work has been asserted in accordance with sections 77 and 78 of the Copyright, Designs and Patents Act 1988.

All Rights Reserved

No reproduction, copy or transmission of this publication may be made without written permission.
No paragraph of this publication may be reproduced, copied or transmitted save with the written permission of the publisher, or in accordance with the provisions of the Copyright Act 1956 (as amended).

Any person who commits any unauthorised act in relation to this publication may be liable to criminal prosecution and civil claims for damage.

A CIP catalogue record for this title is available from the British Library.

ISBN: 978-1-80439-632-2

This is a work of fiction.
Names, characters, places and incidents originate from the writer's imagination. Any resemblance to actual persons, living or dead, is purely coincidental.

First Published in 2024

Olympia Publishers
Tallis House
2 Tallis Street
London
EC4Y 0AB

Printed in Great Britain

Dedication

I dedicate this book to those who have played a part in these poems: family, friends, my partner.

Acknowledgements

Thank you to those whom I have shared these poems with, to those who encouraged me to publish.

Table of Contents

To Write My Love	15
Amazing	16
She Cries, But She Smiles	17
Into You	19
Tonight I'm Whole	20
Also Mine	21
His Arms	22
Innate Inability	23
To Keep This Love for You	24
Tailored Misfortune	26
All I Get	27
Sweater	28
Even Beside Them	29
Mister Snowman	30
Your Eyes' Worth	32
Hold Me Tight	33
Desert of Sand	34
Shapeless Sheet	36

Little Flower	37
Palace Dwellers	38
Who The Fuck	39
Laughter and Wine	40
A Train by Your Name	41
Hold onto Me	42
Eyes Met	43
Naughty Bees	44
Tamed	45
If I Weren't Here	46
Nowhere to be Found	47
White Blood Cells	48
Late Harvest Wine	49
Never Ends	50
Mother Death	51
Fall into Me	52
Sunshine	53
Favourite Profanity	54
The Beauty That	55
The Darkness Hides	55
Yank My Strings	56
Out of the Looney Bin	57
Time Fixes All	58
Cautionary Scene	59

Frown or Smile	60
Green Aventurine	61
Weeping Willow Tree	62
You Became	63
Feel Me Hold You	64
A Million Empty Breaths	65
Spanish Skies	66
I Might Never Learn	68
Thoughts Unwound	69
I Feel Alone	70
Dark Corners	71
It Gets Hard	72
Ceiling	73
Hues	75
Waist	76
Lose Some Sleep	77
What You Had Planned	78
Pebbles	79
My Darling	81
As Completely As	82
Backpack	83
The Rain Has Just Arrived	85

To Write My Love

Had I a way to write my love
Onto this page, I would

For you to understand my love
Perhaps, if read, you could

Alas, no language has the words
To express, to show

What I feel for you, my love
Perhaps you'll never know

Amazing

I'm proud of me for being me, for loving me
And for treating myself accordingly

I'm proud of me for choosing to see
That I am nothing short of amazing!

She Cries, But She Smiles

She cries, but she smiles
And her heart walks for miles,
But she never arrives at her destination
Because she puts others first
So she never walks her way
She's always led the way
By what other people say
Realize that her heart is not a fucking Uber!

And she does care for herself,
But she cares for others more
She's run-down
And she's walked over
So she cannot mend her sores

She smiles, but it's fake
Because other people take
More than she can give
And it's not fake because she is
It is fake because she cannot
Because other people take
Even when she hasn't got

And let me tell you this
When you ask, and she gives
She gives from her heart's abyss
Because she mines herself for others
Until there's nothing but her sorrow
And that sorrow, she hides
So when you ask her tomorrow, and she gives
Try to say, "Thank you", and mean it
And don't take her for granted

Into You

Your strong hand takes hold of my jaw
Your eyes scream whispers from within

And when you put your lips against my skin,
My body, my will, my soul falls into you
Into your control

There are no words, only silence
Loud silence
Unspoken, yet true

My body forgets itself
Becomes a part of you
Becomes a part of us

Tonight I'm Whole

I fall back into your arms
Give myself to you
Having what once was mine
Turning a blind eye to the truth

For tonight is all I have
For tonight our love is new
Though tomorrow I'll be broken,
Tonight, I'm whole with you

Also Mine

When you're sad, love, so am I
And when you come undone and cry,
My bones ache
Filled by tears inside
For you'll never carry pain alone
Your pain is yours, but also mine

For you, my love, I'd tear my flesh
And give to you my dying breath
And when a tear rolls down your face
And softly falls into my hands,
It crashes through my heart and breaks it
Scattered like the desert sands

His Arms

I give myself to his arms
Yet his arms are not the ones
I desire to be inside
But from myself I hide my desires

For my pride would not survive
The truth I hide inside

For the arms I truly wish
To find myself inside
Are the arms that which my pride
Had knowingly left behind

Innate Inability

I turn my eyes from the beauty
Perhaps innate inability
To choose what I know is good for me
Pathetic, you might argue
Well, I agree unreservedly

To Keep This Love for You

I won't chain myself to another
To keep myself from hurting
When the whole relationship is burning
So much deeper than the surface

Every day it's the same
We fight over things that cannot change
And then you give me the blame
I give me the blame

Only to be told:
"Babe, I'm sorry. I was wrong."
"Please, let's stay strong."
"Don't leave me."

So I give you a change
And for a few days we dance
So perfectly to the song of your perfect romance
But only until it ends

And then we commence
With this fucked up routine
So many times seen
So many times felt
In the deepest parts of my broken heart

And here I sit
Blaming myself for the hurt
That I feel towards you
Towards us
And I blame myself for giving up
For not being enough

Today I cut this chain
That chains me to this pain
That makes me cry into the arms
Of the one who does the harm

I will not do this anymore
I will not do this to myself
Though you're the person that I love
My heart cannot maintain
A love for the one
Who puts it in constant pain

If there's one thing that is true
It's that I love you
So much more deeply than I do
Myself

So tell me what to do
To keep this love for you
But I refuse to take the blame
When you are the one
Who sets my love aflame

Tailored Misfortune

I set myself up
Tailored misfortune
Self-sabotage of sensational proportion

Convince myself I'm emotionally well
Run in his direction until
I crash, heart first, into a wall
A wall that I, myself, constructed
Yet headed towards, uninterrupted

A wall I had seen
Right when I started
Yet towards it I darted

With all of my love and all of my hope
With all of my heart
Now nothing but rubble

So I pick up what's left
Start building once more
Higher and stronger than the wall built before

All I Get

Me, this body, this mind, this soul
Is all I get
And it's all that stays
When all else has left

So I choose to love my skin
To see the beauty within
To nurture and respect
To take pride and not forget
To be the person I am truly
Unapologetically me

And to see the simple beauty
Hidden in my smile
To listen to my laugh, thinking,
"Damn boy, that's mine!"

Sweater

Drinking coffee in your sweater while you're sleeping
Cause I don't want to miss a second of this feeling

It's half past two. My eyes are getting heavy,
But you're so perfect, curled up here against me

When you find someone better,
Will you leave me your sweater?
So I can always have this feeling of you

Even Beside Them

We blind ourselves to the ones we love
And assume their mistakes as our own

We learn to tolerate and wear a mask
To hide inside how they break us down

We fail to realize that the bricks of the walls
That they once broke down
Are now the bricks in their hands being thrown

And when all is calm, and the dust settles down
We wake up to realize that even beside them
We are alone

Mister Snowman

So adorable, it's borderline pathetic
Your comments, your looks so sour
Sweet on my tongue, make me diabetic
Give me more I can devour

Go ahead and throw your pebbles
Hard as you can to break me down
Mister Snowman, I'm a hot summer's day
So glare at me with your pebble frown

Throw some more. I'll pick them up
To decorate my garden
A little pebble collection
To make your snow heart harden

I'll greet you with my sunflower smile
Water it with your soggy frown
Make my smile grow ever bigger
While your mood keeps sinking down

Tickle my leaves with your pokey words
Smell my flower smile bloom
Shower onto it, you sad old cloud
I'm delighted by your gloom

Melt away now, ever smaller
Ever less significant
Watch my flower grow ever taller
Ever more magnificent

Your Eyes' Worth

You see my worst
And you see my best
Which in and of itself isn't all that good

You feel my love
Sometimes my lack thereof
Yet my ugly and wrong go understood

Somehow, someway, find something lovely to say
Something beautiful and wonderful about me
And you make me believe in the good that you see

Thank you that I may live in your eyes as worthy
And for pouring your eyes' worth into me

Hold Me Tight

Hold me tight when the wind
Comes blowing against our walls

Hold me tight when the rain
Comes rushing down our shingles

Hold me tight when the hail
Tries to enter through our windows

And hold me tight when the frost
Threatens to freeze our souls

Desert of Sand

Desert of sand upon which I lie
Staring at the moon
Can I reach it if I jump high?
Can I jump if I try?
Can I even move?
No.

So blow your sand onto me
Cover me so I may cease to be
No one cares after all
All have forgotten me
All, even I

If I try, can I get up and fly?
Could I ever reach the moon?
"No, you cannot!" it cries
This desert of sand upon which I lie

Desert vast and wide
Every grain a dream of mine
Every grain cuts into my flesh
As the winds of doubt arise

Desert of sand upon which I lie
Staring at the moon
Desert of sand upon which I'll die
Still wishing I could fly

Shapeless Sheet

We lie in the sweat
Silently
Our bodies no longer one
Our minds worlds apart

We took flight
We crashed hard
We became one
We fell apart

We lie in the sweat
Silently
We stare through one another

Our eyes gone cold
Forgot their colour
Our love unfolds
Leaving lines across our souls

An origami masterpiece
Now nothing but a shapeless sheet

Little Flower

Little flower you are, teasing me with your dance
But then you go and blame it on the wind
Are you scared, little flower, of a little romance?

Little flower, do you wear your petals just for me?
If you want me to take note, to see
Why, then, do you hide so shyly behind your timid leaves?

Little flower, swaying sweetly in the afternoon breeze
Will you with me your sweet perfume share?
Little flower, tell me please, do I pick you?
Or do I leave without you sitting in my hair?

Little flower, how you tease me!
Do you think it fair?
Only to tease, but never to give
How can a simple fellow bear?

Palace Dwellers

Why must he live this life
Eating off of bones
While others dwell their palaces
And sit on golden thrones?

Thrones they were born onto
What wrong did he do
To be conceived in a womb
That birthed him into this lowly place?

How does he uplift himself
When the features of his given face
And the colour of his skin
Are regarded as more important
Than what can be found within?

How do the palace dwellers look at him
And fail to see a human being?
How is he to them a pest
When all he does is his best
To escape an inherited poverty?

Who The Fuck

Who the fuck is this
Person I see
When I look in the mirror
Staring back at me?

What the fuck is this
Life he leads?
How does he live with himself
With his words and deeds?

Why the fuck was he
Placed on this Earth
When all he does
Is cause others to hurt?

Where the fuck did he
Lose his empathy
Not giving a fuck about
Anyone except he?

How the fuck do we
In this body coincide?
How do I peel him off of me
And live from him untied?

Laughter and Wine

Our souls intertwine through laughter and wine
Come find my hand, let your steps lead mine

Confide in me, for I confide in you
We speak our deepest secrets

You lead me to and lead me through
Your inner person, your truest you

And the more you show, the more I know
That you are a soulmate of mine

A Train by Your Name

A train by your name
Rushed through the station of my heart
You barely stopped before you did depart

Now the station lies abandoned
No more than echoes cross the rails

And though many before you did pass,
You had been the very last

And it's been years, yet my heart still fails to open
For when you left so suddenly,
You left my heart so broken

Now every day, I kneel down and pray
That I may join you where you are

And though I'd travel the world for you
We're more than distance apart

Hold onto Me

I'm on a boat in this deep blue sea
Hold onto me, hold onto me

But this boat is made for one only
You hold onto me
He holds onto me
She holds onto me
They hold onto me

Now I'm sinking, too, in this deep blue sea
They hold onto me, hold onto me

This deep blue sea will swallow me
You hold onto me
He holds onto me
She holds onto me
They hold onto me

Eyes Met

Yesterday, our eyes met
In a moment, we exchanged a lifetime
Without speaking a single word
But I felt a tongue-tied coward

I looked away
You left the train
I shouldn't have stayed
But my legs were lame

I hated myself so much
Got off at the next stop
Walked the rest of the way home
Sighing, kicking stones

A life played out in front of my eyes
I blinked and it was lost
Now every time I get on the train
I hope to catch a glance of you
And never look away again

Naughty Bees

Touch my skin, stone in a pond unexpected
Breath in, sensation travels like ripples

Your breeze, honey sweet
Smile at me, bright as spring's blossom

My knees, fallen weak like autumn leaves
Tender breeze carries me closer

Like blades of grass in the wind
Perfect dance, bodies in a trance

Dry as summer heath
Lips bit by teeth

Eyes like naughty bees, stingers dripping
I'm your flower, land on me

Come to me like morning dew
I awake thirsting you

Tamed

This constant cycle that I cannot seem to break
Free from myself

That broken person that I used to be before
I met you

And then you took the time to truly love
Me and my flaws

You endured through the pain
'Til I retracted my claws

You have me tamed
I am yours

Now and forever
Our love be my cause

If I Weren't Here

If I weren't here, my parents would be happy
If I weren't here, my lover would be free
If I weren't here, my friends would have one less burden
If I weren't here, the Earth would keep turning

My parents wouldn't have a son living far away
They wouldn't have to pray
And worry every day

My lover wouldn't have a weight that weighs him down
Where he doesn't want to be
He'd be free

My friends wouldn't need to sit and listen
And give their time
To unimportant problems like mine

This big ball we spin on wouldn't stop without me
Without the extra weight
She would simply be relieved

Nowhere to be Found

If I were to disappear
Would anybody here
Realize that I'm gone?

Would my lover simply move on?
By my family, would I be missed,
Or would they simply forget
That I used to exist?

Would my friends be confused,
Or would they simply get used
To not having me around?
If I were nowhere to be found?

White Blood Cells

Thoughts leave my head
And drift up to the clouds

Touching tall blades of grass
As through the undergrowth they pass

Tiny orbs float in the blue
White blood cells in my eyes, I know

But I choose to see them as the souls
Of every plant and every creature
That once was or roamed

How beautifully they dance together
And I come to wonder whether
I one day will dance with them

Only to be spied by the occasional child
Who takes the time to stare up at the sky

Late Harvest Wine

You breathe your breath like a necklace around my neck
Interlock our fingers, your warm palms grip mine

Your tongue, sweet as late harvest wine
Takes hold of mine and like vines they entwine

Your eyes shine into me an autumn sunrise
Your soft-as-silk sweet strawberry locks

They flow across my face
My heart forgets its pace

I lose myself in the smell of you
And take flight in your perfume

Your voice to me a melody
As you utter your pleasure aloud

Tighter and tighter we are wound
Until we shoot into the clouds

Never Ends

Up and down
Round and round
Hardly touching ground
Lap after lap
Beheaded athlete on a closed-circuit track

Fall down, get up
Succeed, fuck up
Pull ahead, fall back
Never ends, this track

Every day the same
Head racing
Breath racing
Heart racing

Up and down
Round and round
Been here before
Be here again
Never ends, never ends
Run a lap, round the bends
Restart at the end
Again and again

Mother Death

Take me into your arms, Mother Death
Hold me fast evermore
Lay me down and help my soul
To stop hurting ever so

And though I know this life is 'beautiful'
And 'mine for the taking',
I haven't felt it for a while now
And I've gotten tired of faking

So let me fall asleep against your bosom
Guide me to a profound rest
And may I wake to find my body
Lying lifeless on your chest

Fall into Me

Fall into me
Sink.

Open your lungs
No air to breathe

Scream for help
Too deep.

Look up
Light fades to a sliver
Sliver fades to black
Black fades

Suffocate.

Sunshine

The sun shines upon everyone
Sure, but she does so unequally
Choosing to shine more
Upon the offspring of the ones
She shone upon before

Favourite Profanity

Yell your favourite profanity at the bitch in the mirror
Yell the one that makes your mother whimper
Then turn around and walk away
Leave her there to simmer
Leave her there to cook in her own negativity
While you go live and let yourself be free
Let yourself be enough

The Beauty That
The Darkness Hides

The sun sets
Darkness overwhelms the light
I feel a lost child, alone among the monsters of the night

Stars come out
Shine onto me, into my being
I come alive and float towards the beauty

The beauty that the darkness hides
Only to be found gazing at the starry skies
Let them carry you away
To where the monsters take off their disguise

They become friends
They become strengths
They become that which you'd never have guessed

But only if you let them be
Let them open your mind
Let them lead you to find your truest self
Hiding behind the darkness inside

Yank My Strings

Yank my strings
You've tied them after all

Around my arms, legs
Around my mind and my soul

Yank on them until you encounter
A way to make me do that which you desire

Yank until I no longer think
Until my thoughts are no longer my own

Until my actions, my words
Belong wholly to you

Until I am but a puppet, an empty vessel
A ghost under your control

Until you've made me into whom I am not
And whom I do not want to be

Until you come to hate me for not being me
For being that which you've yanked me to be

Out of the Looney Bin

It feels good to be busy again
To be out of my head again
To be out of the looney bin
Or maybe not entirely

But it's good to feel less wound
To feel my feet on solid ground
And to feel a tranquillity this profound
Even if only for a bit
Even if this isn't the everlasting 'it'

It's good to be here
To have my mind this clear
And even though this too might pass
I'll make the most of it while it lasts

Time Fixes All

Time fixes all
So they say

But time is not strong enough
To fix me

Time is not long enough
To fix me

I'm not saying they're wrong
I agree

That time fixes all
All except me

Cautionary Scene

Rip a page from my diary
And convince me of the following
'This day never did exist'
'In fact, it was nothing but a dream'
'And though felt, and though seen'
'Count it as but a cautionary scene'

Frown or Smile

Whether I frown or smile
The grass still dances in the fields
The trees still sway in the winds
The sun still climbs into the morning sky

Whether I frown or smile
The blades still wither in the cold
The trees' leaves still dry and fall
Darkness still returns as night-time arrives

Whether I smile or frown
The world still goes on
So I, too, might as well move along

Green Aventurine

Lying down flat on my bedroom floor
Hand holding tight a magical stone
"Green Aventurine, heal my soul
The lady at the store promised me you will"
She spoke of vibrations and healing properties
So, whether magic or placebo, work on me

Woke up with a sharp pain in my back
I slept on Green Aventurine
Stabbed in the back by a magical stone
And a lady's vibrational healing and so

Weeping Willow Tree

Throw dust into my eyes
So I may cease to see

Pour wax into my ears
So I may cease to hear

Erase my memories
So I may cease to think

Bore a dagger through my heart
So I may cease to feel

Tie a rope to a branch
Of a weeping willow tree

And hang me therefrom
So I may cease to be

You Became

You became my wishing well
Flipped pennies into you
Not knowing yet what I hoped to find
But wishing that it would all come through
I was wishing on a wishing well that's you

You became my submarine
Safety found under the deep blue sea
Not yet knowing where we'd go
But knowing I'd be safe with you
I was safely in a submarine that's you

You became my slot machine
Spent all my time on you
Not yet knowing when I'd win
But to you I was glued
Convinced that my prize would be you

You became my runaway
One day I looked, and you had left
Not wanting what I wanted from you
You did that which you thought was best
And though you left my heart so blue
Perhaps your leaving was what I had needed from you

Feel Me Hold You

When you feel lonely
Or when you feel blue
Put your hand on your heart
And feel me hold you

A Million Empty Breaths

And like smoke you flowed away
I tried to breathe you in
But to no avail

You left, evaporated
Out of my lungs
Out of my life

I lost you a million times
I suffocated a million nights

My lungs without you in them
Again and yet again

A million empty breaths
A million empty nights in an empty bed

Spanish Skies

We lie side by side
Ocean waves crash at our feet
Traffic fades into the sound of Mariachi and Reggaeton

A foreign lust below Spanish skies
Passion erupts in your eyes

My lips in yours lose their minds
The ocean takes control
And washes our burning bodies into rhythmic tides

You incarcerate my tongue
Lock it up with your eyes
Ever mischievous as the night is long

You breathe heavily
Your hands explore
"Calma, chico, por favor"

My fingers flow through your hair, my holdfast
Our breaths dance into humid air
Our bodies burn as the wet tides pass

A stranger awakes in my arms
We greet the morning sun
Has love to me become nothing more than the physical?

I Might Never Learn

What's your name?
I forgot to ask
Last night before I took you home

It's not your fault
You are enough
I am the one who cannot see your worth

Forgive my small talk
This wasn't meant to hurt
You deserve more than my shallow words

I am sorry
I fail to feel more than this
And trying might only make it worse

Perhaps you could teach me
Though I might never learn
To love you after the sun comes up
To love you as deeply as you deserve

Thoughts Unwound

The night swallows the sun
Thoughts unwound become
Mind overgrown by thorny vines
Lies as truths disguised

Nightmares bleed into reality
Reality forgets itself to be
Mind runs uncontrolled
To where fear the power holds

The sun wakes the morning sky
Nightmares run and hide
Lies die, tears dry
Fears fly away

But only until again
The night swallows the sun
Only until again
Thoughts unwound become

I Feel Alone

I feel alone

Your body,
An emptiness beside me
I feel alone

Your breath,
A cold breeze in my neck
I feel alone

Your hand,
A brick on my chest
I feel alone

Your words,
Shards of glass cut through my head
I feel alone

Your kiss,
A flame burns me to death
I die alone

Dark Corners

The dark corners of my mind
Usually stay on their sides

But tonight, they're growing darker
And I find no ray of light

Tonight, they're growing inwards
And they cover up my sight

They make the image hard to see
Hard to make sense of rationally

Hard to be here in my mind
When all its walls close in on me

Hard to reason, try to find
A purpose to everything

Hard to believe all is okay
When a thousand times I've said it

Hard to carry on this way
When I can simply end it

It Gets Hard

Can someone turn on the light?
It gets hard to see
Through the darkness inside

Can someone open this door?
It gets hard to knock
With blood on my fists and knuckles sore

Can someone tell me it's alright?
It gets hard to believe
After the millionth time

Can someone dry these tears?
It gets hard to stay afloat
When the water's up to my ears

Can someone untie this rope?
It gets hard to breathe
With my feet off the floor

Ceiling

The ceiling grows taller
Expansively
Farther away

Echoes of voices dance around the walls slowly
Uncomfortably
Amplifying around me

Light peeks in through the window shyly
Inquisitively
Like a curious child

Dust glimmers as it floats gracefully
Unhastefully
Through the illuminated air

The room starts to spin around me
Slightly
Or is it my head?

The chair in the corner morphs awkwardly
Horrifyingly
Approaching the bed

A weight on my chest holds me down firmly
Frightfully
In my own cold sweat I drown

Then all goes white suddenly
Overwhelmingly
Bright and silent, dead silent

In my hands I hold my head
Desperately
I need this to end

Hues

The sun sets
Your surface reflects the most beautiful hues
Pull me closer
I walk into you

You shine through my eyes
Into my soul
I surrender control
Into you I let go

Wash over my heart with your colours
Wherewith paint it whole
Smile on my face as I go down
Smile on my heart, in you I drown

But your colours do not extend beyond the surface
They fade and reveal the darkness
Much too dark, much too late
Much too cold for me to escape

Waist

Your waist fits so perfectly in my hands
Sending through them waves like electricity
Your waist was made to be held by me

But in your chest there's an empty space
Your eyes stare through me hollowly
Yet your body awakes something within me

Do my hands not awake something within you?
Do I not make you feel the way you make me do?

If I gave you my heart, would it fit?
Would it fill the space where yours used to sit?
Would that make you whole?

Would that set you free?
Free to feel the electricity
Free to let my hands fit so perfectly

Lose Some Sleep

I should pick up your clothes
They're all over my bed

But I can't do that
My heart doesn't know yet

And I can't bring myself to tell it
To tell it that you've left

So I guess I'll lose some sleep
Or sleep in another guy's bed

What You Had Planned

I am sorry
I know I am not whom you wanted me to be
Not even close to what you had planned for me

You turn your face away from me
I disgust you, I'm disgusting
I am sorry

I don't deserve your love
I am unworthy thereof
I ought to change who I am

Or perhaps I am not the one in fault
Perhaps your love isn't loving enough
Perhaps you ought to change

Perhaps the me in your vision you see
Isn't whom I am meant to be

Perhaps what you had planned for me
Isn't my responsibility

Pebbles

All I see, all around me
Are pebbles on a pebbly beach

They're all the same
Nothing special to me

Searching head down
Walking, kicking, rummaging, digging

They're all the same
What now?

Will there be no pebble for me?
A pebble that shines perfectly

The sun sits down upon the horizon
She stares at me with golden eyes

"Found no pebble?" she asks
"Nothing special," I reply

"Nothing special?"
"Mhm"

"My dear, pebbles are pebbles
They're nothing special, that's true

"But it's not the pebble you find
It's the pebble you choose

"And it's not the pebble that shines
It's whether it shines to you"

My Darling

Shut your eyes, my darling
Incarcerate your tears
Your cheeks are too perfect to be blemished by them

Hand on your chest, my darling
Give no power to your fears
Your heart is too perfect to race for them

Hands over your ears, my darling
Their words are spears
Your being is too perfect to be bruised by them

Be your truest self, my darling
And over the years
You'll learn to love your differences from them

As Completely As

I wish to one day love myself
As completely as your embrace loves me
I wish to one day believe in myself
As completely as your eyes believe in me
Teach me, Mother, how to love, how to believe

I wish to one day accept myself
As completely as your smile accepts me
I wish to one day support myself
As completely as your words support me
Teach me, Father, how to accept, how to support

I wish, if one day I have a son
To love, to believe, to accept and to support
As completely as to me you've taught

Backpack

Every word
Ever spoken to me
Other's opinions
Of my body

I put in my backpack
Carried them with me
Yet I never realized
How it weighed on me

It got heavy
Broke my back and crushed me
The pain was so great
That I forgot how to be

The doctor found nothing wrong
Said my pain wasn't real
But x-rays don't see souls
Nor invisible backpacks on shoulders

I am guilty, though
Of listening to others
Of letting them alter me
And of forgetting myself to be

So I guess that now it's up to me
To unpack my backpack
To discern what I need
But more importantly, what I don't

The Rain Has Just Arrived

The first drops bless the soil
Summer has been too long
My garden has been dry
So many flowers have died

So many sunny days have scorched them
So many days I've cried
Attempting to keep them alive
But tears did not suffice

Never mind, the rain has just arrived
My garden smiles and kisses my nose
With a fragrance long forgotten

A raindrop falls upon my cheek
And rolls towards my chin
A raindrop or a tear?
Whatever, does it matter?
The rain is here

Thank you for reading my poetry, now don't let it sit on your shelf.

Share it!